Contents

What is a habitat?

A **habitat** is a place where plants and animals can find what they need to live. Like you, they need food, water, and shelter.

squirrel

HORRIBLE HABITATS
Streets and Alleys

Sharon Katz Cooper

www.raintreepublishers.co.uk
Visit our website to find out more information about Raintree books.

To order:
☎ Phone 0845 6044371
🖷 Fax +44 (0) 1865 312263
🖳 Email myorders@raintreepublishers.co.uk

Customers from outside the UK please telephone +44 1865 312262

Raintree is an imprint of Capstone Global Library Limited, a company incorporated in England and Wales having its registered office at 7 Pilgrim Street, London, EC4V 6LB – Registered company number: 6695582

Edited by Charlotte Guillain, Rebecca Rissman, and Siân Smith
Designed by Joanna Hinton-Malivoire
Picture research by Tracy Cummins and Heather Mauldin
Originated by Chroma Graphics (Overseas) Pte. Ltd
Printed and bound in China by Leo Paper Products

ISBN 978 1 406212 94 5 (hardback)
14 13 12 11 10
10 9 8 7 6 5 4 3 2 1

ISBN 978 1 406213 02 7 (paperback)
14 13 12 11 10
10 9 8 7 6 5 4 3 2 1

British Library Cataloguing in Publication Data
Katz Cooper, Sharon.
Streets and alleys. -- (Horrible habitats)
577.5'6-dc22
A full catalogue record for this book is available from the British Library.

Acknowledgements
The author and publisher are grateful to the following for permission to reproduce copyright material: Age Fotostock p. **20** (© Danilo Donadoni); Alamy pp. **13** (© Don Vail), **18** (© Corbis Premium RF/DLILLC), **25** (© Frances M. Roberts), **26** (© dumbandmad.com); Corbis p. **22** (© Bob Sacha); DRK Photo p. **21** (© Martin Harvey); Getty Images pp. **7** (© Allan McPhail), **9** (© John Downer); Derek Jensen p. **16**; Minden p. **11** (© Cyril Ruoso); Photolibrary pp. **8** (© Tony Tilford), **10** (© EA. Janes), **12** (© Robin Redfern), **17** (© Juniors Bildarchiv), **19** (© DesignPics Inc.), **23** (© Bartomeu Borrell); Shutterstock pp. **4** (© Brian J. Abela), **5** (© Junker), **6** (© Dmitry Remesov), **14** (© Pallando), **15** (© Gastón M. Charles), **24** (© Tobias Machhaus), **27** (© Glenda M. Powers), **28a** (© Keith Levit), **28b** (© Stephan Glebowski), **28c** (© Alex James Bramwell), **29d** (© cbpix), **29e** (© Serghei Starus), **29f** (© Bruce MacQueen).

Cover photograph of pigeons reproduced with permission of Alamy (© Simon De Glanville).

Every effort has been made to contact copyright holders of material reproduced in this book. Any omissions will be rectified in subsequent printings if notice is given to the publishers.

Some words are shown in bold, **like this**. You can find out what they mean by looking in the glossary.

There are many types of **habitats**. Forests, ponds, and fields are all habitats. But even a street can be a habitat.

This dark alley is a habitat.

Out on the street

Rats are common street animals. They live close to humans because people leave old food and yummy rubbish for them to eat.

Rats will eat mouldy or rotting food.

FUN FACT

A group of rats is called a **mischief**.

9

Rats **urinate** or wee as they run around. This leaves a trail that other rats can follow. We can't see these trails in the dark, but other rats can smell them!

FUN FACT

Rats go to rubbish bins at night for a delicious snack. They sometimes find dog poo there to munch on.

A street could hold thousands of rats because they have babies very quickly. One female can have three to six **litters**, or sets, of babies a year. Each litter could have at least 12 babies.

rat babies

Rats can carry many **diseases**.
Diseases can make people
ill or die.

13

Hair for dinner?

Stray, or homeless, cats wander around alleys. They eat rats. They also spend a lot of time licking their own hair to stay clean. They swallow some of that hair.

A cat's tongue is rough. This helps the cat to clean itself.

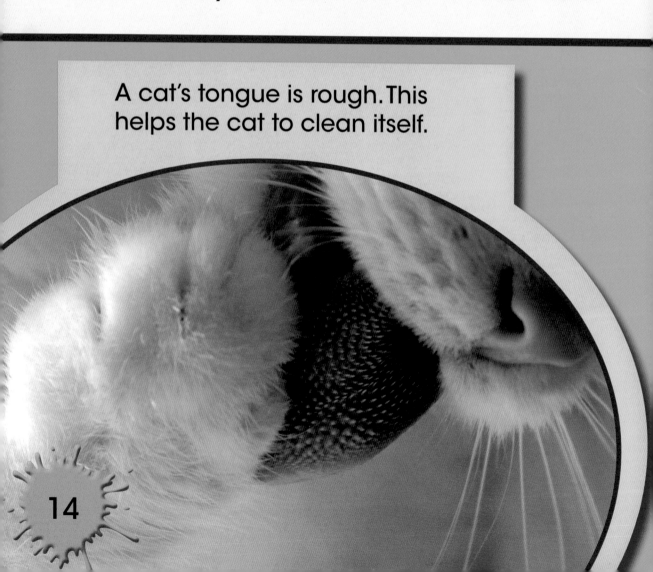

Hair vomit!

Swallowing hair is a problem for cats. They can't **digest** it or break it down, so it forms clumps in their stomachs. Then they vomit it out. Yum – hairballs!

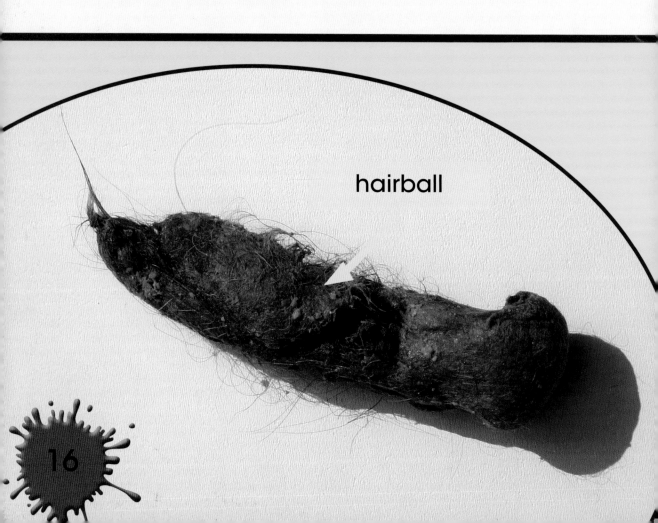

hairball

Rabid raccoons

In some countries, raccoons slink around alleys. They are good climbers. They climb over fences and up the sides of rubbish bins looking for food.

Raccoons use their own wee and poo to mark the places they think of as their own. These places are called **territories**.

NOT-SO-FUN FACT

Some raccoons carry the **disease**, or illness, rabies. So if you see a raccoon, stay away!

Cockroaches' favourite places

Cockroaches are famous street creatures. They live in sewers during the day. At night they scurry into the street to look for better food.

Cockroaches don't like the light. They prefer dark places like this hole.

Cockroaches eat rotting food and human poo. They also eat grease from stoves and glue under the labels of cans. They even eat fingernails and hair from people!

In this cockroach poo you can see some of the things the cockroach has eaten.

Scavenging birds

You may see many birds in city streets. Some birds such as crows and seagulls are **scavengers**. This means they will eat what they can find. They will even eat bits of other dead birds.

This crow is eating a dead pigeon.

Large numbers of pigeons live in city streets, too. Pigeons eat almost anything, including rotting food.

Hungry squirrels

Squirrels run and jump all over streets and lawns. They eat seeds and nuts. They will also poke around through rubbish bags for leftover human food, bugs, and even dead animals.

Squirrels chew on branches to sharpen and clean their teeth. They chew on power lines for the same reason. Sometimes this causes the power to go out in nearby houses.

If they can find chips, street squirrels will eat these too.

27

Street matching

Which of these animals would you not find in the streets? Note: not all of these animals are in this book.

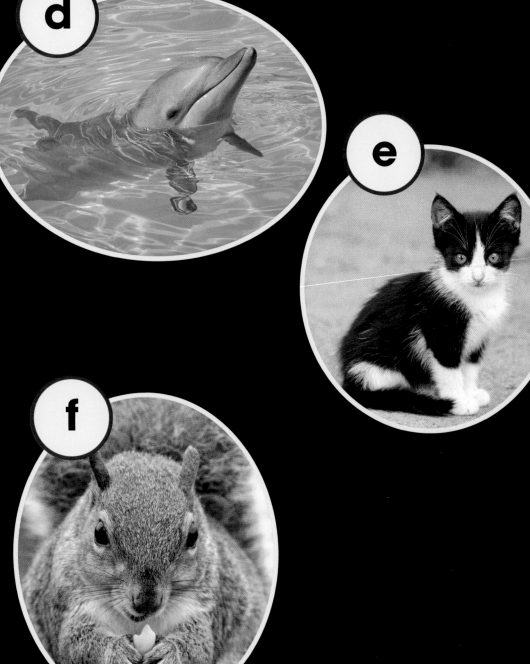

d

e

f

Answers:
You would not find the lion (a)
or the dolphin (d) in the streets.

Glossary

digest break down food into small pieces that the body can use. Animals usually digest things in their stomachs.

disease illness

habitat place where animals or plants live and grow

litter group of babies born at the same time

mischief group of rats

scavenger bird or other animal that feeds on waste and other dead animals

stray animal without a home

territory area that an animal thinks of as its own

urinate wee

Find out more

Find out

Why is the rhinoceros cockroach famous?

Books to read

Animal Neighbours: Rat, Stephen Savage (Wayland, 2007)

Bug Books: Cockroach, Karen Hartley, Chris Macro, and Philip Taylor (Heinemann Library, 2008)

Habitat Explorer: City Explorer, Neil Morris (Raintree, 2004)

Websites

http://www.bbc.co.uk/nature/wildfacts/factfiles/190.shtml
This website has lots of pictures and information about squirrels.

http://www.pestworldforkids.org/rats.html
Find out about different kinds of rats on this website.

http://www.nhm.ac.uk/kids-only/life/life-small/cockroaches/
Find out some fascinating facts about cockroaches on this website.

Index